HOW TO END POVERTY IN THE WORLD IN JUST 15 YEARS

Jean-Pierre Twagirayezu

authorHOUSE®

AuthorHouse™
1663 Liberty Drive
Bloomington, IN 47403
www.authorhouse.com
Phone: 1 (800) 839-8640

Published by AuthorHouse   07/07/2017

ISBN: 978-1-4389-0707-9 (sc)
ISBN: 978-1-4685-3494-8 (e)

Library of Congress Control Number: 2008907169

CONTENTS

THE SOLUTION TO THE PROBLEM OF POVERTY IN THE WORLD

INTRODUCTION

Today the countries of the world can be divided into two main groups. The first group is composed of those often called *developed* or *industrialized countries*. The people living in these developed countries have a high degree of entrepreneurship, and they create all kind of companies that give high-paying jobs to the population. Agriculture is highly mechanized and uses modern technology, which greatly increases productivity. In these developed countries almost all children have access to education until at least high-school level, and the students who are very motivated can attend university. These countries are also characterized by the availability of health care covering the majority of the population. A great majority of the population in these countries lives in cities. Although some of these developed countries experience a higher level of unemployment, the majority of the population in them live in conditions of relative prosperity.

The second group of countries is comprised of countries often referred to as *developing* or *third-world countries*. These countries missed the industrial revolution that stated in Western countries in the eighteenth century, and industries are still almost nonexistent in them. The vast majority of the population lives in the countryside, where they subsist by growing crops or breeding domestic animals on small family landholdings. The population of these countries is locked in poverty because the land they exploit is too small, and it hardly permits them to produce enough food to feed their families. In these countries only a small portion of all the children are able to attend high school, and a very small minority are able to attend university. Besides farming, some very small businesses that mainly consist of small boutiques, and the relatively few government positions, very few other jobs exist. The majority of the population has limited access to modern health care, and these countries are also characterized by a high level of infant mortality. Roads are in very poor condition, and very few of them are paved. A great number of people live in extreme poverty, in cramped housing without running water or electricity.

THE VICIOUS CIRCLE
OF POVERTY

The majority of the populations in developing countries are farmers, who subsist by exploiting the meager land they own. These farmers are uneducated, and they practice farming using rudimentary techniques. Because they exploit small plots and don't use modern techniques of farming, such as using fertilizers and pesticides to combat crop diseases or selecting the most productive breeds of their domestic animals, these farmers are hardly able to produce enough to feed their families, and they take what little surplus remains to the market. These farmers stay poor for their whole lives, and because they have little income, they have limited buying power.

When an entrepreneur starts a factory, for example, only a tiny portion of the population, perhaps 5 percent, will be able to buy regularly what that factory produces. This factory will have a very small market for the product it makes; this will keep the factory small and enable it to employ only a few people. Also, this factory will have to pay very low wages to its employees in order to be able to make products that will be affordable for the population. Since any factory that is created in a developing country has to be small and pay very low wages to its employees, such a factory will hardly be able to address the problems of unemployment and poverty. This is because it cannot employ many people, and the few people it employs earn very low wages and continue to have low buying power. Some countries try to attract foreign companies looking for cheap labor and interested in producing goods for export. But because these foreign companies are looking for cheap labor, this means that they also will pay low wages to those they employ, and these people will never get ahead in this case as well and will remain poor.

When the government wants to undertake any project, like building a road or a hospital, bringing clean water to a remote region of the country, building a school, etc., it must rely on loans from the IMF or the World Bank, which carry very high interest. But because of the chaos and corruption existing in these countries, they are never able to repay their loans, and this further burdens their economies. The government cannot collect enough taxes from the population, and thus it has very little revenues. Except for certain developing countries which export some kind of commodity like oil, precious minerals, coffee, sugar etc., the governments in most developing countries have very limited revenue. Even the countries that export commodities don't make much progress because the prices for these commodities on the international market are very low, and these countries do not receive deserved revenues. Even when commodity prices are high, these countries do not have the appropriate economic policies and use the income obtained not to invest in production but to import foreign products that are sold to the population, and this way, these countries also make little progress.

As things are today in developing countries, you cannot create a large factory that will give jobs to a lot of people, because a large factory will produce too much for the available market. Since not enough high-paying jobs can be created to offer workable alternatives to farming (which might release land on which extensive and modern farming can be practiced), this means that the people living in these countries will continue to live in extreme poverty. So how to raise the standard of living in developing countries to something more comparable to that in developed countries? In what follows we are going to address this problem.

THE SOLUTION TO THE PROBLEM OF POVERTY IN THE WORLD

1.

THE ROLE OF MONEY IN THE ECONOMY OF A COUNTRY

Across the world today, money is given prime importance whenever you want to do anything. If you need food to eat or clothing to wear, if you want a house to live in, if you need to get married, if you need to send your kids to school or to buy a car, if you get sick and need medical treatment, if you need transportation to go to work—anything you want to do requires money. It is common for people to say that money rules the world.

When any government wants to undertake any kind of project, it needs money. In developed countries, the money needed by the government to put in motion its agenda comes from the taxes paid by the businesses and the working population of those countries. In poor countries, the working people with good jobs and the ability to pay fair taxes to the government amount to only a tiny percentage of the whole population. Also, only few businesses can pay enough money to the government so that it may undertake projects to benefit the whole population. In developing countries, the government has very little revenue because the source of revenue is very narrow, and this situation renders the government unable to undertake projects that could benefit the whole economy of the country, like building needed roads, providing clean water to the population, bringing electricity to the whole country, building needed schools and hospitals, and creating the infrastructure needed for rapid industrialization. Anytime a government of a developing country wants to do something, it has to contact the IMF or the World Bank for a loan, because it has no resources of its own. And because the needs of developing countries are vast, the loans that these countries receive from the World Bank and the IMF will be insufficient. Indeed, the money needed to build the whole infrastructure necessary to allow rapid industrialization of developing countries is so vast that the World Bank and the IMF would run quickly out of money if they were to provide the right amount of money necessary to end poverty in developing countries. In most cases also, even the small loans approved by the World Bank and the IMF are mismanaged by the government of developing countries, which in most cases are plagued by corruption. As a result, such loans never produce any substantial result, and these countries always have trouble repaying the loans.

2.

WHERE THE VALUE OF MONEY COMES FROM

We have just seen that whether a person or a government needs to undertake any project, it needs money. But where does the value of money or currency come from? We all know that money comes always in the form of a piece of paper or metal, emblazoned with specific and complicated designs, to which the government assigns a specific amount. If a specific piece of paper, or *bill,* shows the denomination of 100 units of currency, for example, it means that this bill has a value of 100. The person who owns this bill can exchange it for a good or service to which a seller has given the value of 100.

The bill in itself has no value and is a simple piece of paper, unless the government guarantees that it is covered by goods and services equivalent to the amount written on it. If you have a thousand bills that are marked 100, you are 100,000 units of currency richer. Depending on the value of the currency in the country you live in, you can buy a car, build a house, go on vacation, etc. This means that the *value* of the thousand bills you have, each worth 100 units of currency, is given by the *amount of goods and services* you have access to because of that amount of money. If the price of these goods and services goes up, you can buy fewer of those goods and services with your thousand bills. This means your money will have lost value; this is called *inflation*.

Also, in order to be in possession of the thousand bills, unless you have stolen them or they are a gift, you have to have done something (produced something or provided a service) valued at 100,000 units of currency. There is no other way you can be in possession of that money. If it is a gift, the person who gave that money to you needs to have done something of good value to obtain it. If it is a loan, you must have shown the ability to repay the loan, or in other words, the ability to produce something useful worth 100,000.

In any case, we can see that the value of money is always given by the amount of goods and services it covers. But the goods and services covered by money are produced by the work of the people who put their efforts into producing them. It is the efficient work that produces goods and services that gives value to all the money circulating in any given country. At the end, then, *it is efficient work that gives value to money.* The more a population works efficiently, the more high-quality goods and services are produced by the population; the more money is put in circulation by the government; the more money is earned by individuals in that country and the richer the whole population is in general. If the government puts in circulation an amount of money that far exceeds the amount of goods and services produced by the country, there will be inflation because fewer goods and services will be covered by too much money, and the price of these goods and services will go up, leading to the loss of the value of the money. This situation is seen in the economies of many developing countries, where the value of a unit of currency can sometimes be far less than that of a unit of currency in a developed country.

As we have just seen, it is efficient work that gives value to money because it is efficient work that produces useful goods and services. **By** *efficient work,* **I mean** *high-quality and productive work, achieved through constant innovation and improvement and good management.* The harder a great percentage of the population works efficiently, the more goods and services produced, the more money earned by the population through high-paying jobs, the more tax paid to the government by businesses and individuals, the richer the population, the richer the country. I have to mention here that a highly educated population will be highly efficient in its work.

The degree of efficiency differs from country to country, and we can see that the most powerful country in the world today, the United States of America, is mainly characterized by a very high degree of efficiency. High productivity is achieved through the extensive use of computers and superior technology. Sound management also promotes constant innovations and improvements to bring new products and services to the market, where they are promoted with good marketing. Creativity is very high also in the United States, and all these factors combine to create a society where unemployment is usually low and where high-paying jobs are common. One consequence is that all the material needs of the population are mostly met and the country enjoys relative prosperity.

Work in developing countries, on the other hand, is mainly characterized by low efficiency. Farmers have little land to exploit and use rudimentary technology, mainly their physical strength, to do their work. They use almost no fertilizers or pesticides and therefore produce barely enough to feed their families and put any surplus into the market. These farmers, who constitute the vast majority of the population, remain poor their whole lives. Industries are almost nonexistent, which means the whole population has very low income. Even those who work for the government are paid low wages, since the government has very little in the way of resources.

3.
MONEY IS ONLY AN INSTRUMENT OF DISTRIBUTION

From what we have already seen, we can conclude that it is *efficient work* that produces the goods and services that constitute the wealth of a country through the transformation of raw material and not money itself. Money is only a tool that allows people to exchange the goods or services they have produced. Money is only an instrument of distribution. First, useful goods and services are produced; second, money comes in to help people exchange and distribute those goods and services produced, according to each person's needs and capabilities.

Let us say, for example, that you work in a factory making shoes and you are paid the equivalent of US$240 a month. However, you need food to feed your family. Since you make shoes, you produce something useful to others, and you are paid for it. To buy food, you will have to spend part of your salary for these expenses. Let's say you spend $20 to buy food. In this case you have used part of your salary to access the service provided by the grocery store. Since the grocery store has been able to sell its products, it will be able to pay its employees as well. An employee of that grocery store will be able to buy a pair of shoes you make.

Also, you don't need food only; you may also need clothing. If you spend $3 to buy a shirt, you will be paying part of the salary of those who made the shirt. A person who worked on making the shirt will be able to spend the money he earns according to his needs. He could decide, for example, that he wants to buy a bicycle if he can afford it. By buying a bicycle, he will be providing money to the people who built that bicycle, who themselves can go ahead and buy food, shoes, and clothing, pay for transportation, etc. The more people work, the more customers businesses will have, and the exchange of goods and services through money will go on smoothly. The more the businesses are *efficient*, the better the salary they will be able to pay their employees, and the more prosperous the population will be.

As we can see, first there is always the production of a useful good or service through efficient work, and the person who performed that work is paid money that he uses to have access to the goods and services produced by others. *The key is the production of useful goods and services first, through efficient work of some kind, and money comes in later.*

Consider the case of the United States. If somehow you wiped out all the factories and the agricultural activity of the country, all of a sudden the dollar, the most powerful currency in the world, would begin to lose value. Inflation would follow, because all of a sudden there would be fewer goods and services available for sale to the public. Since the few goods and services available would be needed by too many people who have money, the price would go up quickly, and the dollar would lose a great part of its current value.

The weak dollar would also do no good when it comes to importing goods from other countries. Because the economy supporting it would have collapsed; nobody would want it. This would worsen its declining value, and the American people wouldn't be able to buy enough goods to meet their needs. But the dollar wouldn't collapse totally. There would remain the abilities and the talent of the American population for rebuilding the lost infrastructure and activity. If, in addition to wiping out all factories and all farming activities, you somehow were to take away all the talent and skills of the American people, America would become a third-world country like any other, and the vast quantity of dollar bills circulating all over the world would become almost like ordinary paper.

Although different tenders like credit cards, checks and electronic funds transfer are used today in the process of exchanging goods and services; all these tenders act like if they were physical currency and there are considered like another form of representing money.

All that I have mentioned in this chapter is intended to deemphasize the role of money in the economic activity of any given country, and to emphasize the role of *efficient work* that produces goods and services as the true engine that drives the economy and as the *true starting point of the economic activity of a country.*

In order to solve the problem of poverty, we are going to show how efficient work can be brought to any given country, no matter how poor it is. Vigorous economic activity can be launched in even very poor countries, with previously little economic activity to lift whole populations out of poverty and into prosperity.

4.

LAUNCHING THE ECONOMIC MACHINE OF ANY COUNTRY

In past chapters, I emphasized the role of efficient work as the true starting point of the economic activity of any country. But efficient work means work of good quality that is done with high productivity and good management. Obviously, efficient work means industrialization, since only work done in a factory with machinery and proper technology can have high productivity and good quality. High productivity and good quality mean workers will be paid an acceptable salary, a salary that will allow them to meet all their material needs and stay out of poverty. If the factory built in a developing country does not have enough productivity—for example, if an employee of a shoe factory can only make one pair of shoes per day, this means that this employee has very low productivity and will be paid a very low wage, given the selling price of that pair of shoes. This means that even if this employee has a job and is working in a factory, he will never get ahead and will remain poor, so this will not solve the problem of poverty.

But high productivity means the production of a large amount of goods and services in a short time by comparatively few employees. If, for example, a shoe factory is to contribute to easing the problem of poverty, it must have an acceptable number of employees compared to the size of the population. If this factory has high productivity, this means that a large number of shoes will be produced each month by that factory. For this factory to be profitable and remain in operation, it needs to mass-produce shoes, and the shoes produced need to have buyers. The main problem faced by developing countries is the fact that the few factories built there have few customers for their products. This means that such factories employ fewer people and pay them low wages because of low productivity, which does not ease the unemployment problem.

In order to have highly productive factories that mass-produce useful goods, we need to have a sufficient number of buyers for those goods. This means that we need to have a large number of the population who have a regular income and can buy the products. But for the population to have regular and sufficient income, it must have good jobs, mostly in highly productive factories and services.

The solution to this dilemma is to start with a massive industrialization of the country from the very beginning, and also start with factories that produce essential goods—those that everybody needs—to ensure success. **Such massive industrialization, involving a large number of factories, at once ensures that a large proportion of the population will have regular and acceptable income and constitutes the market for already existing and future factories. This situation will allow intensive exchange of goods and services through money to begin.**

Assume, for example, that a certain country has a population of 60 million people. If 1,000 factories that employ in average 3,000 people each are started, we will suddenly have 3 million people who have regular income and can buy goods and services produced by others. If we consider that each working person has a family of six, we will immediately have 18 million regular consumers. Since these 1,000 factories will be serving a population of 60 million and will have a base market of at least 18 million persons, they will be able to use the latest technology for high efficiency and productivity. This means that they will be able to pay a good salary to their employees; thus, the 18 million people will have a good buying power. If we consider the number of services that will be associated with these factories; such as retail stores, restaurants, public transportation, telephone companies, banks, schools, hospitals, insurance companies, government entities etc., we can add easily another 10 million people who will have good regular income because of this nucleus of 1,000 factories. This means up to 28,000,000 people who will have good buying power—nearly half of the nation's population.

These 28 million people will need homes to live in. Since we have considered a family of six, this means we will have to build 5 million homes or apartments on average. The homes to be built will need to be modern in every way, with all the equipments found in homes in an industrialized country. Such homes would present many advantages: The appliances to be installed in these homes would all have to be made inside the country. This would mean jobs for the people who work in the factories that make these appliances. These factories would be part of the first nucleus of 1,000 factories.

Consider, for example, the factories to make cement, iron reinforcing bars for concrete, iron ore, steel, bricks, wood, doors, bathroom sinks, bathtubs, windows, tables, chairs, doorknobs, glass, electrical washing machines and dryers, electrical stoves, microwave ovens, refrigerators, electrical lighting equipment, floor tiles, carpets, paint, mattresses, bed sheets, televisions, portable radios etc. We can see that a large number of factories will be associated with home building and furnishing alone. For these factories associated with home building to be successful, they need to have a large market for what they produce. This means that a huge program of home building can be undertaken. *The larger the number of homes that are being built simultaneously, the larger the number of equipment to be put in these homes, the larger the market for the factories that make such equipment, and the larger the number of high-paying jobs created.*

If, for example, a program of building 250,000 homes every three months is undertaken, and if we assign an average of ten people to build each home and estimate that it would take on average three months for the ten workers to finish building each house (always using modern technology and modern techniques), we will have 2,500,000 more people with good jobs and a regular good income. If we consider a family of six for each person, that means that 15 million more people will have a good buying power, and a total of 43 million people have access to the market already. The rest of the population who constitute the workforce of the country (here we are excluding underage and elderly people who cannot take a job) could be employed in farming, and this activity would have to be modernized as well so that their small numbers could produce enough food for the population. A large number of factories producing food-related products, such as factory production of chickens and eggs and modern raising of pork and cattle for the production of meat and all kinds of dairy products, would be started as well, and these industries could be part of the first nucleus of 1000 factories. If we consider a family where the husband and wife both work, the household income would be greatly increased. This will be common, since jobs will be abundant in different economic sectors that we have not mentioned.

But the great question everybody is asking right now is—where to find the money to build these factories? The answer is these factories would be built by foreign companies from industrialized countries. In other words, these factories would be built through a process of globalization done the right way. The government would begin by planning and organizing the whole process. After the government has put the steps to be taken in order, it would begin to persuade an experienced foreign company for the product it wants to be made in the country to come and build the factory. The government can give incentives to the chosen company, such as a partial monopoly on the market and guarantees that the product produced will be sold or that the government will cover any loss.

The government can also guarantee a fixed percentage of net profit to each company invited to do business in the country, such as a 20 percent (of the cost of production) net profit on each product made. This way, the companies coming to do business in the country would have a clear vision of the potential for growth at hand. And since they would have first claim on the market, they would be sure that their 20 percent net profit would be met every year. Any product made inside the country would no longer be imported.

It would be wise to invite only two companies for each product to be made. This would limit competition as well as overproduction and the price wars that sometimes complicate the business environment, and each company doing business in the country would have clear vision and would grow steadily, without difficulty. The government should establish a system of control to make sure that no company goes beyond the 20 percent net profit level. In the event that a local entrepreneur has enough capital to start a certain factory, he would be given priority.

An experienced company with enough capital to come to put a factory inside the country would be invited to manufacture any desired product. Such companies would build factories to make cement, steel, bricks, glassware, electrical or gas stoves, dishwashers, washing machines, dryers, microwave ovens, electrical equipments, bathtubs, bathroom sinks, plumbing equipments, soaps, towels, clothes, shoes, toothpastes, wood furnishings, TVs, portable radios, carpets, bicycles etc. Companies that specialize in agriculture and farming would be invited as well, in order to modernize this sector, and these companies would use the land vacated by the people who took manufacturing and construction jobs. This will have made available the opportunity for efficient work, the driving force of the economy of a country. *By inviting foreign companies to come to do business inside your country, you quickly gain access to both modern technology and experienced management at the same time.* Famous companies like General Electric for electrical products, Whirlpool for home appliances like washers and driers, Colgate Palmolive for toothpastes and toothbrushes, Hanes for the making of all kinds of underwear, Dove for the making of soaps, Lafarge for the massive production of cement, Sony or Samsung for manufacturing all kind of electronics like portable radios, TVs and cellular phones, ArcelorMittal for the production of steel —all these great companies could be invited to do business in the country. And with all the incentives and guarantees they would be given, they would not hesitate, since these kinds of companies don't have any problem with the capital needed for the investment.

It is best if the whole manufacturing process can be done inside the country whenever possible. Also, priority should be given to the types of products for which the raw materials can be found inside the country. Such products will be preferred to those using imported materials. Whenever a natural resource can be used to make a product, it will be preferred even if the product may have lower quality. For example, if metal, plastic or wood can be used to manufacture a certain product, wood would be preferred because the needed trees can be easily grown inside the country. This practice will fortify the economy and will allow the creation of a nearly closed economy. This means that *all goods and services produced inside the country are the product of the workforce of that country with the introduction of foreign technology*, and this will have a great importance, as we will see later.

This process also will allow for proper use of the funds obtained from export. If there is, for example, too much importation and not enough exportation, the country will suffer from a trade deficit, which will hurt the economy. I have to mention that this type of economy would rely on the internal market rather than on export, and this will create a robust economy because the internal market can be easily controlled by the government. And since most governments could adopt this economic plan as well, it could be hard to find manufactured products that could be exported.

Relying on the internal market will allow the government to fix an acceptable minimum wage that will allow everybody to have good access to the goods and services produced inside the country. This kind of industrialization differs from the type of industrialization driven by the availability of cheap labor and mainly focused on exportation. This last kind of industrialization hardly addresses properly the problem of poverty, because indeed companies that come to do business in the country pay very low wages. As a result, the population has no way of accessing the goods produced, because they are expensive and destined for export.

5.
PARTICULARITY OF THIS NEW ECONOMIC MODEL

The way money is printed and put into circulation

The economy must revolve around home building and furnishing.

In order for the government to ensure success in implementing this economic plan, it needs to have full control of the process of printing money and putting it into circulation. Instead of putting money into circulation through random loans given by the central bank to the government and other banks, the government can use a better brand-new process that is as follows:

The economy would revolve around home building and furnishing, and each quarter, the central bank would *print* the amount of money equivalent to the total number of modern homes built and furnished. Let's say that 250,000 homes have been built with furnishings in the first quarter of the year. If, for example, the companies that built these homes are selling each house for $24,000, the central bank would **print** the amount of money equivalent to the value of the homes built, which is $24,000 x 250,000 = $6,000,000,000, and loan it to realtor banks inside the country. Realtor banks would have the task of buying all the homes built and making them available to the working population through long-term loans. Banks would be instructed to ask just $2,000 of interest on each home loan of $24,000 for the whole duration of the loan. This means that bank would ask $26,000 for each home, and the buyer would have to repay through monthly installments or mortgage.

By buying each modern home built for $24,000, the bank would be supplying the money used to pay the workers who built that house, as well as the money used to purchase the materials used to build it, all the modern equipment inside it, and the profit of the company that built it. If, for example, 250,000 homes have been built and in each one there is a drier and a washing machine, which have a combined cost of $400, this means that $100,000,000 from the money loaned to realtor banks went to the business that makes driers and washers, and the 6,000 employees of this company were paid money that originated first from the central bank or the government. This is true also for the employees of the cement factory, bricks factory, windows and glass factory, floor tiles factory, carpet factory, electrical installation equipment factory, mattress factory, and the makers of all the other furnishings used in the homes.

All the workers of these factories were paid the money *printed* by the central bank and loaned to realtor banks, which used it to buy the homes. The workers of these factories will use this money to buy all the goods and services they need, and these products will be available because of the existence of the nucleus of 1,000 high-productivity factories. In no time, then, money will reach the 43 million people representing the six-member families of all those who have a job. The home building and furnishing was chosen because of the large number of jobs associated with this activity and because it is a product of first necessity, a product that every family needs. Also, living in a nice home is the symbol of the end of poverty, and this is what everything is all about.

In order to make it easier for foreign companies to build new homes inside the country, the government could provide low interest loans to these companies so that they can be able to pay their employees as well as buy locally produced supplies. This way, these foreign companies would not have to invest too much of their own money in the process of building these homes. Once they finish building the homes, they would sell them to realtor banks and then be able to repay the loan they took from the government.

The foreign companies coming to do business inside the country would then provide modern technology and know-how, but any local material needed and the cost of the labor could be covered by money loaned to them by the government.

The whole process will be as if the government is buying the goods produced throughout the country and selling them back to the population through low-interest loans. If high-quality goods and services have been produced in the country, these represent wealth that has been created. This represents an increase in the Gross Domestic Product (GDP). The government can then afford to *print* money equivalent to the goods produced and put it into circulation to allow proper exchange of these goods and services among the population. The government should have no trouble in covering the goods and services produced inside the country, since *everything will be done using mainly the raw materials found inside the country*. This means that all the products would be the result of work performed by the workforce of the country, employing foreign technology introduced through foreign investment, and this will allow the government to have full control of the circulation of money in the economy.

In cases where a large quantity of imported material is needed to manufacture enough needed products in the country, this could be a problem since there may not be enough exports to generate the hard currency necessary to buy those imported materials. This is why it would be very important to use locally produced raw material first, whenever possible.

6.
CREATING WEALTH WITH A PROFIT

When a business is in operation, it must be producing a needed product or service. If a company is making shoes, for example, the value of the shoes produced each day must be greater than the cost of producing those shoes. Suppose that the factory has 70 employees and it is able to make 1,000 pairs of shoes each day. If the average wage for each employee is $2.00 per hour, and each employee is working 8 hours per day, this means that the cost of labor to manufacture 1,000 pairs of shoe every day is $1,120. If the cost of the material necessary to make those shoes plus other expenses is $500, the total cost of producing those shoes will be

$1,620. If the factory can easily sell each pair of shoes for $2, it will be making $380 of net profit every day.

This means that the 70 employees of this factory, in addition to being able to draw their salary each day, generate a profit of $380 each day they work. These workers have been able to produce something useful that constitutes wealth and have been able to generate a profit as well. If we have numerous factories like this one, wealth is being created every day and a profit is being gained every day. If the cost of living for each employee is less than what he is earning, this employee is being paid well for what he does, and he is making a profit himself with the salary he earns. Because wealth is being created with a profit, things keep rising; people get richer and richer, and it keeps going on and on.

The central bank needs to ask for some interest as well on the money it lends to realtor banks to help them buy the new houses. The central bank can ask for $500 of interest on each $24,000 it lends to a realtor bank. Since the bank is going to ask for $2,000 of interest on each home loan it provides, this bank will not have any trouble paying the $500 of interest asked by the central bank. In this case, when a person is beginning to repay his mortgage, the initial payments would cover the interest owed to the bank, which is $2,000. As the bank is paid its interest, it can quickly pay the central bank its $500 interest.

This $500 is money earned, because everybody who is working is generating a profit for himself and for the company he is working for. Since the central bank would be under the control of the state, this would mean that for every 250,000 homes built, the state is earning a profit of $500 x 250,000 = $125,000,000. This means that every three months, the state is making $125 million dollars of profit. This amount of money can be used by the government to finance all kinds of projects that need to be done, or for some developed countries, it can be used to help people move into new houses, if they still have a portion of a mortgage to pay and the house they live in is too old or is not comfortable enough according to the standard they have set. When realtor banks pay the principal of the loan to the central bank, this money is simply destroyed because it has finished its job of facilitating the exchange of goods and services among the population.

The central bank would keep lending money to realtor banks, and realtor banks would keep buying the homes built. The focus would always be around the interest that realtor banks earn and the portion of earned interest that realtor banks owe to the central bank. If everybody is working efficiently and is being paid a good salary, this system will keep going, and people will get richer and richer.

7.

REPAYING THE HOME LOAN OR MORTGAGE

We have mentioned that this economy would be based on efficient work. This means the work is done through high-productivity factories offering high-quality goods under solid management, employing modern technology. Since the workers would have high productivity because they would be using modern and appropriate technology, they can be paid high salaries because their output would be high as well. In this economy, a minimum wage equivalent to US$1.50 an hour could be established, and all businesses would be able to at least pay this wage to their employees, because they would have high productivity and customers for the product they massively produce. A person earning $1.50 an hour would make $12 in an eight-hour day and $60 a week (if he works only five days per week) or $240 per month. With such a monthly income, this person could afford to dedicate at least $90 each month to repaying the home loan. With the payment of $90 each month, this person would need twenty-four years to repay the $26,000 that the home cost. This is an acceptable time frame for repaying this loan, since it commonly takes up to thirty years to repay a mortgage loan in developed countries. If both the husband and wife have a regular job to help pay off their house, it would take even less time to repay the home loan.

In this process of home mortgage payment, when the person who took the loan becomes unable to pay or when he dies before he has finished paying off the loan, the bank simply takes the home and sells it to somebody else. The leftover money after the bank has recovered its outlay belongs to the family of the person who was living in that house. The bank incurs no risk at all.

Every person having a job generated by this economic plan (who would earn at least the minimum wage) would then be able to afford to buy one of the modern homes that are being built.

But are the minimum wage of US$1.50 per hour and the $26,000 price for each home reasonable? Let's take the example of the workers who build houses. We estimated that it would take ten workers three months to build each house. Since each worker would be paid $12 per eight-hour day, we can see that the ten workers would be paid $120 per day, $600 per five-day week, $2,400 per month, for a three-month total of $7,200. The cost of labor to build each house would then be $7,200. If the material to build each house cost $5,000 and its furnishings cost $8,000, we can see that it would cost $20,200 to build each house. If we fix the profit of the company that built the house to be $4,000 and the interest of the realtor bank to be $2,000, we can see that this home can be sold to the public for $26,200, and anybody earning the minimum wage would be able to buy this house and fully pay for it in just twenty-four years, as we've seen already.

The home building business could be a very interesting one, and anybody who knows how to build modern houses could ask for a loan in a bank and begin building houses for sale to the public through realtor banks.

8.
Obstacles to This Economic Plan

The first obstacle to this economic plan would be the shortage of skilled workers. If you want to build 250,000 modern homes every three months, you need to have a large number of workers who know how to build modern homes. This is the same situation for the people who would work in factories. They need to have skills.

The solution to this problem would be, in the case of home building for example, to begin by building small numbers of homes in order to train workers. You can begin, for example, with a program for building 10,000 homes or apartments. The workers who built these first 10,000 houses would gain experience and skills, and the next step would be to build 20,000 houses. This means more unskilled workers would have been injected into the home building business, and they would be trained by the workers who built the first 10,000 houses. The next stage might be to build 40,000 homes, and the number would keep growing until enough workers became available to build the 250,000 homes.

Also, the first nucleus of 1,000 factories wouldn't be built and ready to operate at full capacity overnight. The process of building these factories would go on gradually, with priority being given to the most fundamental factories (factories for cement, bricks, and steel, for example). The most important factories would be built first. All factories would be built with high capacity (enough capacity to serve a population of 60,000,000 people with good income), but they would not function at full capacity from the very beginning. They would increase their production gradually, as more and more homes were built and the industrial buildup continued. It could take five to seven years to have the first nucleus of 1,000 factories in place and operating at near full capacity.

It is very important not to think in terms of money first and be impressed by the large number of homes to be built every quarter (250,000 houses or apartments). As we have seen in past chapters, the important thing is to start with a large number of factories almost simultaneously, and the rest can be for the government to **print** money and put it into circulation. Since goods and services of high quality will have been produced, the government can afford to put money in circulation that will cover the value of the goods and services produced.

Also, some people may say that many third-world countries have totalitarian rulers and are plagued by corruption, and so this new economic model will not work. I have to say that even though it is preferable to see all countries of the world ruled under the principle of democracy; this new economic model can be launched even in countries considered to be under dictatorship. Sometimes countries under such regimes are put under economic sanctions, and it is only the people who live there who suffer, while they are powerless to do anything to change the regime. I believe that there is some goodness in everybody, and even dictators will accept this plan, provided that their grip on power is not threatened; in this way the population can be saved.

Concerning corruption, the main reason for it is because of the general situation of poverty that the people are living in and the lack of opportunity. Those who have some kind of position that allows them to provide a needed service to the public try to exploit it to the maximum. As the situation improves and poverty diminishes, and abundant opportunities appear, people tend to be more honest, and corruption decreases.

But the most important obstacle to this economic model is the shortage of energy in the world. It has been seen how the price for crude oil has risen from less than US$20 per barrel in the year 2003 to more than $100 in 2008; and this rise was mostly caused by the rapid industrialization in China and India. If all the developing countries could experience the same pace of industrialization, the price of a barrel of crude oil could easily hit $200 within a few years. Very few countries can afford to buy oil at $200 a barrel, and this means that alternative sources of energy to fossil fuels must be found.

One alternative source of energy could be ethanol produced from corn. Each developing country can then undertake a program of growing corn on a large scale for the production of ethanol, which can be used to power factories and automobiles. Another source of energy to be considered could be the harnessing of wind to produce electricity. Solar energy is also an alternative, but this technology needs to be refined first so that it can be exploited efficiently. But the ultimate solution to the problem of shortage of energy around the world is a free energy producing machine that I have invented and which I call *ENERGY MACHINE*.

The Energy Machine produces mechanical energy without consuming any raw material and indefinitely. This machine is easy to build and it can be of any size depending on the power output desired. It is possible to manufacture at very low cost a small Energy Machine that can provide energy to any household. It is also possible to manufacture heavy-duty Energy Machines for industrial use. The Energy Machine can be also installed in trucks, buses or cars to replace today's internal combustion engine. The Energy Machine will be the main source of energy on this planet in the near future.

With the Energy Machine, the problem of energy around the world is solved, as well as the problem of global warming, because the Energy Machine does not produce any emissions.

I know you may be very skeptical right now about the feasibility of a machine capable of generating useful mechanical energy without any kind of input. However, I have been able to have an expert in physics scrutinize the theory on which the Energy Machine is based, and this physicist could not find a reason why the machine wouldn't function as expected. This physicist used to teach mechanical engineering courses at one prestigious American university.

I am currently trying to find the money necessary to build a working model of the Energy Machine.

The transition to free energy should be made as smooth as possible, and companies involved in the production of energy could be given the opportunity of switching to manufacturing all kind of Energy Machines. Also, Utility companies involved in the distribution and the sales of energy to the public could be the ones given licenses to sell manufactured energy machines to the public. This way, no company would get bankrupt because of this new technology.

Countries that produce and export energy related commodities wouldn't be affected negatively by this new technology either, because they can be able to diversify quickly their economies with the help of this new economic model. In latter chapters of this book, I will present more advanced ideas that will help any country achieve the status of a developed country in a short period of time.

With the Energy Machine comes the possibility of dismantling the existing electrical grid in the near future, allowing to release beautiful landscapes which were previously hampered by power lines.

Also, with free energy, it will be possible to purify ocean water and use it to irrigate previously unfertile lands like deserts and transform them into fertile lands on which extensive farming can take place and produce food for the people.

In addition to solving the problem of energy, I intend to use this invention in order to sustain this new economic model as follows:

9.

WHERE THE INVENTION OF THE ENERGY MACHINE COMES IN

I intend to create a licensing company that will give other companies the right to manufacture all kinds of Energy Machines, and these companies would be paying me a good royalty. *With this in mind, it is then possible to create a trillion-dollar company* from the royalties received and from the appreciation of the stock of this company on the stock market. How to use all this money? *The best way to use this money may be as* **insurance** *for any company from a developed country which accepts this economic plan and agrees to come and do business in even the poorest countries in the world today.*

The insurance would work as follows:

– I have said that one of the incentives that governments should give to foreign companies is a partial monopoly on the market. Also because it would be easy to track the number of people with good and regular income, companies would have good visibility and would be able to manufacture the right quantity of products to be put on the market. Companies would then be able to correctly estimate their potential net profit, which should be 20 percent of the cost of production. If, for reasons other than the company's own incompetency, a company does not meet at least 75 percent of its projected profit, the insurance would kick in. If, for example, a company makes only 60 percent of its estimated profit, the insurance will give the company a sum of money equivalent to the 15 percent of net profit it was unable to earn. Any company that accepts this plan then would have the assurance that it will always make 75 percent of its projected earnings. The main acceptable reason for claiming this insurance should be the absence of buyers for the products made, and a system of controls should be set up to make sure no company inflates its potential earnings.

– The company I intend to create should not have any problem in providing insurance coverage for all companies doing business in developing countries all over the world according to this economic model. I intend to call this company *Enermach Corporation.*

10.
GUIDELINES FOR PUTTING THIS ECONOMIC PLAN INTO MOTION

FIRST STAGE

– The first step for putting this economic plan in motion is to identify the areas within the country where factories will be built and areas where residences and services will be established. Residence areas and factories areas should be separated by only a few miles so workers may move between these areas using buses powered by Energy Machines.

- The next step is to start building roads leading to and connecting these areas.

- The following step is to bring electricity and clean water to these areas.

For these steps we just mentioned, the government could contact the IMF or the World Bank for a loan, or the Enermach Corporation could provide the loan. Foreign companies that specialize in building roads or building water-sewage installations could be invited as well to perform these tasks.

- In addition, researchers need to evaluate the real potential of the country. Some countries have certain commodities they export, and others manufacture products that could be exported but are not because of ignorance. Some countries, for example, produce exotic fruits and vegetables that are very expensive in developed countries, but the producing countries never export them.

SECOND STAGE

- It is necessary to determine the types of houses or apartments that are appropriate for the country. Architects, both foreign and domestic, should be consulted in older to advise on what kind of houses or apartments to build and to help decide the ratio between houses and apartments to be built in the country.

- Also, this stage should include the creation of an Industrialization Committee. This committee should consist of economists, engineers, and accountants, some of them foreign, and its job would be to identify the industries that need to be started first and to persuade foreign companies to come build these industries inside the country. Members of this committee would present to foreign companies the package of incentives the government is offering and would explain the whole plan to foreign companies in older to assure them of their success if they agree to do business in the country. The work of this committee would be permanent, and it would continue its effort until the first nucleus of 1,000 factories with an average of 3,000 employees has been reached (I am taking reference on a country of 60 million inhabitants).

Members of this committee would travel abroad often, visiting industrialized countries in order to see what kinds of products are sold the most and what kinds of products are used by the general population the most. They would also visit homes in order to see what kinds of necessary equipment are inside. This would give them a good idea of the industries they need to invite in their country.

– Also at this stage, land must be identified that will be vacated by the people who will take the new jobs to be created. It is necessary to decide where high-efficiency agriculture and farming need to be established and to move the farmers occupying those lands to factory jobs first.

THIRD STAGE

- A minimum wage of $1.50 an hour would be established for the people who have jobs directly created by the implementation of this new economic model. If a new factory is being built because of this plan, the workers should be paid at least this minimum wage.

- The currency of the country should begin to be gradually adjusted and increased in value as the economic buildup progresses. The currency should be ultimately adjusted so that the money paid as the minimum wage in local currency is equivalent to US$1.50 per hour. This minimum wage could vary, since some countries could afford to pay a higher minimum wage. No country, however, should establish a minimum wage that is less than US$1.50 per hour of work.

- A system of tax collection would be established, and the government would begin to collect taxes from the new businesses related to this economic plan. The money collected by the government would be used to begin building schools and hospitals, to bring clean water and electricity progressively to the whole country, and to continue to improve the infrastructure necessary for economic growth.

– The school curriculum should be revised so that students are taught the skills they will really need on the job. Some developing countries insist, for example, on mathematics and physics in the curriculum, and any student who fails those disciplines is rejected from the school. These disciplines, however, are only suitable for students who have talent for science and engineering. Students who have talent for other disciplines should be separated from those who have talent for sciences. for them, other disciplines like business management, accounting, social sciences, nursing, etc., should be included in the curriculum as well.

11.

WHAT HAPPENS AFTER FIFTEEN YEARS, WHEN ALL NECESSARY HOMES HAVE BEEN BUILT?

If we consider a country of 60 million inhabitants, for example, and if we estimate that each family has six members, we can see that it will be necessary to build 10 million new houses and apartments. If a program of building 500,000 new homes every six months is undertaken, it would take up to ten years to build all the necessary houses. If we estimate the time it will take to train new workers and the time it will take to have all manufacturing factories built and operating at near full capacity to be seven years, it is clear that after seventeen years all necessary homes could have been built. All the manufacturing capacity that has been developed may now be useless, as the demand for manufactured goods related to home building and furnishing would decrease dramatically.

It is possible to think, then, that after seventeen years of implementing this new economic plan, there would be high unemployment, companies would be bankrupt, and the economy would collapse. I think the solution to this problem would be to gradually move workers from manufacturing jobs into service jobs. This can be done because, for example, in the United States, manufacturing and construction jobs constitute only 17 percent of all existing jobs, and 83 percent of the workforce is in the service sector. The majority of manufacturing jobs have been moved overseas, mostly to China. Until very recently, meanwhile, unemployment in the United States was hovering just around 5 percent of the whole workforce.

Since this new economic plan mimics the economy of the United States, after twelve years of implementing this new economic plan; the Industrialization Committee would begin to focus on starting new service companies. It would try, for example, to invite service companies from the industrialized world that it finds suitable for the country, and ask them to come to do business inside the country. The economy would then begin to switch from a manufacturing and construction economy into a service-based economy. The school curriculum would be established with this in mind also, so that students could learn the skills that would be truly needed by the economy in the near future. Manufacturing and construction jobs would then diminish, and the factories would begin to reduce their capacities. Because the companies which own these factories would have made a lot of profit during the boom of manufacturing (20 percent net profit guaranteed), they would be able to shut down capacity without incurring substantial losses.

Another word I can say about the near future is that I don't think people will continue to work full-time jobs, let's say by the year 2040. When I observe the latest innovations in digital technology, I see an android-like robot that can perform almost 80 percent of the work done by humans today. I think that in the near future it will be possible to fabricate machines that will have humanlike abilities, and these androids will take over up to 80 percent of the jobs done by humans today. So, by the year 2040, I think that humans will be working only part-time, perhaps two to three days a week, and then they will be spending six months at the beach vacationing.

For this to be possible, a surplus of people will be trained to do the jobs that cannot be performed by androids, and they will alternate their time on the job. These androids will be able to work twenty-four hours a day and seven days a week. In this way, there will be greater productivity, and people will be able to earn full-time salaries even if they will be working only a few months per year. Governments will have to charge very high taxes to the businesses that use androids, and then money will be funneled as subsidies to businesses that still use humans, so that people can still earn full-time salaries even if they work only part-time.

12.
NEW ECONOMIC
MODEL FOR DEVELOPED
COUNTRIES

**Creating Jobs through New-Home Building
and furnishing.**

From what I have discussed until now, it is
clear that I was always referring to the poorest
countries in the world today. In fact, while
writing the previous chapters of this book, I
had in mind countries like North Sudan and
South Sudan, Democratic Republic of Congo,
Mauritania, Swaziland, Burma, Bangladesh,
Cambodia, Nigeria, India, Indonesia, Colombia,
Argentina, Chad, El Salvador, Mexico,
Venezuela, Brazil, South Africa, Philippines,

Thailand, Burundi, Rwanda, Senegal, Niger, Haiti, Ivory Coast, Ghana, Cuba, Honduras, Kazakhstan, Uzbekistan, Nepal, Chile, Bolivia, Jordan, Palestine, Malawi, Syria, Iran, North Korea, Iraq, and Afghanistan. Although the degree of poverty is not the same in all the countries mentioned above, most of them are characterized by a low level of industrialization, and a great portion of their population lives in extreme poverty.

I think that the new economic model we just discussed is suitable for all the developing countries that bear the same characteristics as those mentioned above. But how about developed countries that have problems of high unemployment like Spain, Greece, France, Portugal, Italy, Poland, Ukraine, Bulgaria, Romania, Hungary, and Russia? If this new economic plan is able to lift out of poverty an extremely poor country like South Sudan in a little more than fifteen years, it can help solve with greater facility the economic difficulties existing today in developed countries.

Let take, for example, the case of Spain and France. These two mentioned countries have been struggling with high unemployment for decades. Today, the unemployment rate hovers at around 10 percent in France and 25 percent in Spain. This means that, in France and Spain respectively, there are around 3 million and 5 million people who can't find a job. While economists see this large number of unemployed people as a big problem, I see it as a sign of opportunities that are ready to be exploited.

Since France and Spain are industrialized countries already, I think that it would be very easy for them to solve the problem of unemployment by adapting this new economic model to their own economies. With 3 million people looking for a job right now, for example, it follows that there are at least 3 million people who need a decent home or apartment to live in. It is impossible to live in a nice home when you don't have a job and are living on welfare.

The government of France can right now undertake a huge program of putting each unemployed person in a very nice home. Just as we discussed while referring to developing countries, the government of France can put in motion a program of building 100,000 homes and apartments every three months. If we estimate that it would take a group of ten workers three months to completely build each home, it would take 1,000,000 workers to build these needed 100,000 homes.

Just with the number of people who would be hired to build these homes, the unemployment rate would be reduced by 1,000,000 people. But the homes would still have to be fully furnished with all the equipment found in today's modern homes. At least 500,000 more workers would have to be hired to manufacture all the appliances and equipment that a nice modern home requires.

After the unemployment rate has been cut in half, people would begin to feel a sense of security and confidence, and they would tend to spend money they earned more freely. This means that even companies and services whose businesses are not directly related to home building and furnishing would see increased business activity. They in turn would tend to hire more workers, and consequently the unemployment rate would be reduced further. This increased business activity would begin to feed on itself, and the economic growth would be substantial, ending the current situation of economic stagnation.

But where to find the money necessary to build that large number of homes?

Although I touched on this question in previous chapters, I find it necessary to emphasize again the process by which the means to put this huge home-building program in motion are obtained. Since France is an industrialized country already, there would be no need to persuade foreign companies to come to put new factories in the country or for Enermach Corp. to provide industrialization insurance. The European central bank can just *print money out of thin air* equivalent to the amount needed to build 100,000 new homes in France.

By money printed out of thin air, I mean money printed arbitrarily, without taking into account changes in the GDP. That money would then be injected into the economy in a way that would allow it to generate an increase in GDP equivalent to its value. This way, there is no inflation or any other negative consequence because of this new money.

Money printed out of thin air would be loaned to the central bank of France, which would then loan it to private banks in France. Private banks would have instructions to lend that money to home-building companies. The home-building companies would then be promised that after the homes are built, they will be bought by realtor banks—using, again, money loaned to them by the central bank. Once realtor banks have taken ownership of newly built homes, they would sell them to people who need new homes, like the 3,000,000 people who were previously unemployed. These people would now have high-paying jobs generated by the home-building program.

The central bank of France would then get money printed out of thin air from the European central bank equivalent to the cost of building 100,000 new homes and apartments. Once that amount of money was put in circulation through the home-building program, there would be extra economic activity that could not have existed without the central bank putting these new funds in circulation. If we estimate, for example, that each new home cost $130,000 to build, this means that $13 billion would have to be printed out of thin air and put in circulation.

Although this money would be printed out of thin air, it would generate economic activity that would not have taken place without it. These extra activities represent wealth that has been created—meaning that this arbitrary printed money would be covered by goods and services produced because of it. This money printed out of thin air would then have value because of the extra goods and services it helped to generate, which are equivalent to its value. The injection of this new money into the economy would result in an increase in GDP equivalent to its value.

For example, if a private bank loans $130,000 to a construction company, this company will be able to use the money to order cement, iron reinforcing bars for concrete, steel, bricks, floor tiles, drywalls, paint, bathtubs, bathroom sinks, electrical equipment, windows, doors, furnaces, furniture, mattresses, dressers, stoves, washing machines, dryers, refrigerators, etc. The companies that make these products would use the money received from the construction company to pay their employees' salaries and also their suppliers.

The employees who work for the companies that supply material to the construction companies could then use the money to buy anything they need in their daily life, like food for their families, gasoline for their cars, monthly payments on the home or the car they are financing, clothes, shoes, and TV service. Even if the $130,000 loaned to the construction company was originally money printed out of thin air by the European central bank, it has been transformed into useful good and services. The money has moved through all the sectors of the economy of France, facilitating the distribution of goods and services it helped to create.

Once a home has been built, the construction company can sell it to a realtor bank for, let's say, $165,000. The construction company will have made a profit of $35,000 on the home it built. The construction company can then pay back to the private bank the $130,000 it was originally loaned plus $11,000 interest, keeping only $24,000 profit. The private bank that received a $130,000 loan from the central bank would then be able to pay back that loan plus $1,000 interest and keep only $10,000 profit.

Once a realtor bank has purchased a house for $165,000, it can sell it to an individual person who has a job for, let's say, $180,000. This person can then repay the loan through monthly payments. The realtor bank would also have received a $165,000 loan from the central bank for each newly built home it purchased. The realtor bank would then make a $15,000 interest, and it would be able to pay a $3,000 interest to the central bank and keep $12,000 profit.

Alternatively, after the construction company that built the home has sold it to a realtor bank for $165,000, it can use $130,000 out of that money to build another home instead of repaying the loan it got from a private bank. After the new home has been built and sold to a realtor bank for $165,000, the construction company would have made $35,000 in interest, out of which it could be able to pay $11,000 to the private bank and make another $24,000 profit on the newly built home. This way, the original $130,000 loaned to the construction company could stay in the economy, allowing the construction company to use it to build new homes over and over again.

Every three months, the European central bank would print out of thin air $16,500,000,000—equivalent to the cost of buying 100,000 newly built homes—and loan it to the central bank of

France. The central bank of France would then loan that money to realtor banks, which would buy newly built homes and sell them to the public through monthly payments.

If we estimated, for example, that a worker who builds homes in France is paid $15 per hour, this employee will make $2,400 per month, supposing that he works only forty hours per week. This employee could then be able to easily make a monthly payment of $600 on a home loan. It would take this employee twenty-five years to fully pay his $180,000 loan.

For this economic model to work perfectly, it would be very necessary to have buyers for the homes and apartments that are being built. For this reason, once this economic plan has been put in motion, it would be necessary for every person who was previously unemployed to buy a new home and to begin making monthly payments.

The interest that I estimated banks should receive for their services seems small, but I think that it is fair. Banks would be using money directly loaned to them by the central bank, and there would be no risk involved at all. This is because, should things go wrong, the central bank can simply write off the loan, as the money used for the loan was originally currency printed out of thin air.

Surprising consequence of this new economic model:

No need to repay the principal of the home loan.

The central bank would charge a small amount of interest on the loan it provides to realtor banks so that they can buy the newly built homes. Since, as in our example, the central bank would be asking for $3,000 interest on each $165,000 loan it provides, the realtor bank that received the loan would be left with $12,000 profit. In the process of mortgage payment, the money paid is used first to serve the interest on the loan. The person who is making a $600 monthly payment will then need twenty-five months to finish paying the $15,000 interest on the loan. After twenty-five months, the person who took the home loan would begin to make payment on the principal of the loan, which is $165,000. After twenty-five months, the realtor bank will have gotten its $15,000 interest and been able to pay the $3,000 interest it owed to the central bank.

So after twenty-five months of mortgage payments, the money that the homeowner continues to pay to the realtor bank would be transferred directly to the central bank so that the homeowner could fully finish paying off the loan. But an important question that comes to mind right now is this one: what will the central bank do with the $165,000 once it is paid back? Remember that this was money originally printed out of thin air. As this money comes back to the central bank, a nice home has been built and extra useful goods and services have been produced and consumed.

So what will the central bank do with this money as it comes back? In previous chapters, I mentioned that when this money is paid back to the central bank; it is simply destroyed, because it has finished its job of creating and facilitating the distribution of goods and services across all sectors of the economy.

But why should someone who bought a home have to keep paying money to the realtor bank for more than twenty-two years only to see that money destroyed once it reaches the central bank? Simply put, once the interest on the loan has been paid, there is no need to keep making payment.

Once the realtor bank has gotten its $15,000 interest, and once it has paid the $3,000 of interest it owes to the central bank, the central bank can simply write- off the principal of the loan ($165,000) that the realtor bank owed it. The person who took the home loan would not have to make payment on the principal of the loan, and he would be able to keep his home for good.

The business of the realtor bank is to make money, and it would have been able to make its $12,000 profit. The company that got a loan in order to be able to build the home would also have made its profit of $24,000 after selling it to a realtor bank for $165,000. This home-building company would then have been able to repay the $130,000 loan it got from a private bank, plus $11,000 interest. The private bank would also have been able to repay the $130,000 it received from the central bank plus $1,000 interest, keeping only $10,000 profit.

The central bank would have made the original loans to private banks in order to facilitate jobs creation and to build homes for the people, and this objective would have been achieved as well.

The money injected into the economy would have generated extra goods and services throughout all sectors of the economy, and these goods and services would be permanent, whether the principal of the loan was repaid by the home owner or not. All companies and businesses involved in this process would then have achieved their goal. So why would the new homeowner continue to make payment on the principal of the loan? It is not necessary at all.

I just showed that after paying interest on the home loan, buyers would have no need to repay the whole loan, because everything would have started with money printed out of thin air. This money would have been put to work paying people and creating extra goods and services that wouldn't have existed otherwise. This is, of course, different from the case in which someone obtained a mortgage loan from a private bank in which the bank used money earned the hard way, through its own business operations. In this case, the private bank cannot forgive the principal of the loan because it would quickly go bankrupt and go out of business.

All homes-builders would be instructed to use money loaned by the central bank. This way, they would have enough funds to undertake the construction of a large number of new homes at the same time, making them huge profits. But wouldn't it be unfair for the people who get jobs through this new economic model to be forgiven from paying the principal of their home loan while the rest of the population has to spend more than twenty years repaying a mortgage?

I think that in order to overcome this injustice; a system of leverage can be established in which the people who get homes through this new economic model continue to pay a small portion of their home loan. The money would be funneled to a fund that would help people who got loans under traditional terms repay their mortgages. This way, it would be as if people were helping one another pay their mortgages.

With the possibility of not having to repay the principal of the loan comes the possibility of destroying all homes that are very old or not comfortable enough according to the new standards and building new ones that are spacious and more modern. If we consider the case of France with its 3 million unemployed people, there certainly must be at least 3 million more people living in homes that are very old or inadequate. All these substandard homes can be destroyed and new ones built.

A family that was living in an inadequate home and decided to move into a new home would only pay the interest on the loan corresponding to the new home. After paying for the new home, the family could keep making payments on the old mortgage, and the old home would be destroyed.

Injecting money printed out of thin air into the economy in this way would not bring any negative consequences like inflation, deflation, or economic recession. This money would be loaned directly to businesses capable of transforming it into useful goods and services. Everything would be along the same lines as a business taking a loan in order to expand its operations as it sees a new market for the product or service it provides. The population would be able to gain access to the money injected in the economy by working jobs. Everything would seem like the old way of doing business, except that everything would have started with money printed out of thin air.

High economic growth would follow from this new method of stimulating business activity, and the country would experience economic prosperity. Economic stagnation would be a thing of the past. This method would continue on for a while; it would take up to fifteen years to build those 6 million new homes in France, if we consider that only 100,000 new homes can be built every three months. As a result, there would be fifteen years of high economic growth and prosperity. We will discuss later what would happen after fifteen years.

The Case of the United States of America

What I just discussed in this chapter applies to developed countries that are struggling with the problem of high unemployment and economic stagnation. But what about countries like the United States, Japan, and Germany that have relatively low unemployment?

If we consider the case of the United States, for example, we can see that although this country is characterized as having higher economic activity, creativity and salaries, there is still a large portion of the population who live in houses and apartments that are very old and inadequate by modern standards. The United States can therefore also easily start a program of building a large number of new homes and apartments using money printed out of thin air.

Once the homes have been built, people who live in inadequate housing can be presented with the opportunity to move into brand new and modern homes. These people would then be required to pay only the interest on the loan corresponding to the home. Once the realtor bank that provided the loan has received its interest, the principal of the loan can be written off. The realtor bank would not have to pay anything to the central bank. The person who moved into a new home could then continue to pay the rest of the mortgage corresponding to the old home that has been destroyed.

No need to pay income tax

In the United States, a large percentage of money collected by the government through income taxes is spent on three programs: Medicare/Medicaid, Social Security, and the military. Since the majority of people who receive Medicare and Social Security benefits have reached retirement age, the government could simply use money printed out of thin air to finance these programs.

If we consider, for example, the case of Medicare, we can see that if the government sent checks printed out of thin air to elderly people who need medical care, these people would be able to buy the drugs they need and pay for doctors and hospitals services. The pharmaceutical companies that make drugs needed by elderly people who are on Medicare would still have customers for the drugs they make. It would be business as usual for these companies. The same would happen with hospitals. Doctors and nurses and other employees would still do their jobs as usual, and they would still be paid for the service they offer to people under Medicare.

The money printed out of thin air would move through the economy as if it was money collected through taxes, and there would be no economic activity lost. In fact, there would be greater economic activity because people in the workforce would have more money to spend, as they would not be paying income taxes.

Since the people who receive Medicare are already retired and don't participate in the creation of goods and services that compose the economic activity of the United States, giving these people money printed out thin air to pay for their health care wouldn't harm any sector of the economy. Goods and services would continue to be produced, and there would be even more buyers because without the burden of taxes, people would have more money to spend.

You may ask: Why can't the government send money printed out of thin air to everybody? If the government sent money printed out of thin air to people who are still working and participating in the creation of wealth, those people would tend to work less, and many would even quit their jobs. The economic activity of the country would decrease considerably. There would then be too much money in circulation and fewer goods and services to cover that money. This would lead to high inflation, and an economic crisis would follow. Remember, it is efficient work that gives value to money. If efficient work decreases, money loses value, and poverty settles in.

Any action the government can take that will not decrease the economic activity of the country—that is, the production of goods and services—is always welcome. If an action taken by the government increases production of goods and services, and those goods and services have buyers, it is even more welcome. This is the case of using money printed out of thin air to fund Medicare and Social Security benefits. Since the people covered by these two programs are already retired, giving them money printed out of thin air to cover Medicare and Social Security benefits wouldn't cause any decrease in economic activity. Economic activity would rather increase because people who work jobs would have more money to spend, as they wouldn't be paying taxes. They would buy more goods and services, resulting in the creation of new jobs and increased profit for businesses.

The same logic applies to money spent on the military. If the government used money printed out of thin air to finance the military budget, this money could be used to pay the salaries of soldiers and other military personnel. These soldiers would spend this money as usual, and they would be able to buy goods and services they need. The economy would continue to function as usual.

Money printed out of thin air could also be used to buy military equipment from contractors. These contracting companies would use the money to pay their employees and to buy raw material needed to fabricate needed equipment. Using money printed out of thin air to finance the military budget would represent no lost economic activity. Rather, it would increase economic activity, because people would have more buying power as they are no longer paying income tax.

Since the economy of the United States is highly diversified, with all economic sectors highly developed (meaning that the economy is very efficient), any action the government can take that will not decrease the efficiency of the economy but rather increase economic activity is welcome. The elimination of the income tax is such an action. All government expenses can be covered using money printed out of thin air. The farming sector, manufacturing sector, services sector for example, would experience increased business activity, and the companies involved would have to hire more people. Profits would greatly increase as well.

The key here is to make sure that people who are still young and who comprise the workforce of the country remain motivated to take jobs and work. It is their work that creates the wealth that gives value to money. If, for example, you began to give free money to the employees of companies like McDonald's or General Electric, people would quit their jobs en masse, and this would lead to a decrease in goods and services generated by the economy. High inflation would follow, because there would be too much money circulating in the economy while fewer goods and services were being produced. We will see later how people can be freed from having to work at jobs altogether.

I've described steps that the United States can take, but even developed countries with high unemployment can do the same, provided they have first stimulated their economies through the building and furnishing of new homes. When a country has high unemployment and is experiencing economic stagnation, economic activity inside the country is very low. There are many sectors that are not performing in a satisfactory way. Using money printed out of thin air to cover government expenses would put a heavy burden on the limited number of people who have a job.

As described earlier, money printed out of thin air would be loaned to companies that do business related to home-building, and those companies would hire more people. More goods and services needed by the population would be produced, resulting in the creation of millions of new high paying jobs. People would then be earning more money through their jobs. Once the economy has fully recovered and started to grow again, the government can think about decreasing taxes.

But how about corporate tax?

I think that it would be unwise to eliminate corporate tax. This new economic model would generate huge growth for companies and businesses. If these companies were forgiven from paying taxes, the huge profit they make would simply be used to pay exorbitant salaries to CEOs and other executives as well as to fund executives' perks. I think the right thing to do would be to keep collecting corporate tax and use it to fund programs like education or to help people repay mortgages acquired under the old terms.

Solving the problem of the national dept of the United States.

At the end of the year 2016, the United States national debt was approximately $19.8 trillion. The amount owed to foreign investors was about $6.2 trillion and the intergovernmental dept was about $5.4 trillion. Although the size of this dept is very impressing and indeed astronomic, it is possible to pay for it using money printed out of thin air. In order to pay the 6.2 trillion owed to foreign investors for example, the government of the United States can negotiate with foreign creditors a process through which American companies can undertake huge development projects equivalent to the amount owed inside those creditor countries.

Since the amount owed to China is approximately $1.25 trillion for example, the government of the United States can undertake a program of printing out of thin air $200 billion per year, and loan that money to selected American companies, with instructions to start development projects inside China. Those selected companies would use that money to buy all the supplies they need inside United States, and then ship them to China in order to develop the projects they are undertaking there. These American companies could for example start building modern housing for low income Chinese citizens or modernize agriculture in some rural area of China. By undertaking projects equivalent to $200 billion each year, the 1.2 trillion dollars owed to China can be fully paid in just six years.

The same process can be followed in order to pay for the debt owed to others countries like Japan, Saudi Arabia, Brazil etc. and with the ability of the United States economy to transform any amount of money printed out thin air into useful goods and services, United States wouldn't have any problem paying that huge dept in a few years.

Concerning the 5.4 trillion intergovernmental debt, since most of it is owed to the social security trust fund, this dept can simply be ignored because the social security program can be funded using money printed out thin air as we have already discussed.

All the debt owed by the government of developed countries can then be paid using money printed out of thin air which is injected in the economy by loaning it to companies capable of transforming it into useful goods and services. These goods and services would then serve as payment to creditors.

13.

A PERFECT SOCIETY
ON EARTH

A perfect society on earth is a society where harmony, peace and love reign. Harmony has two aspects: material harmony and ideological harmony.

Material harmony means that all the material needs of the people living in all the countries of the world are fully satisfied. The standards of living in all countries of the world are the same. The harmonization of wealth all around the world would lead to less isolation of countries and more and more contact between people living in different countries. Consequently, people would tend to think the same way and have the same values, as they would be living under the same economic and political conditions and there would be frequent contacts among them.

This situation would lead to ideological harmony all over the world, and borders between countries would become increasingly meaningless and obsolete. It would increasingly seem like the world was composed of only one country. This new situation would lead to eternal peace all over the world.

Once material and ideological harmony has been achieved, it becomes possible to eliminate the need for a visa in order to travel from one country to another. For example, we can see that today, the United States, Canada, and most countries of Western Europe have a treaty that allows their citizens to freely travel between them without the need for a visa. This is possible because the standards of living are almost the same among those countries, and their political and economic systems are very similar. There is a high degree of harmony among those countries, and this allows free movement among their citizens.

Harmony among Western countries has allowed them to form a military treaty (NATO) in addition to eliminating visa requirements among their citizens. Today, for example, it is an unthinkable situation that the United States would be at war with Canada, or Germany with France, or the United States with Western Europe. These countries have rather formed a military pact in which they commit to defend each other if attacked.

If we could achieve full harmony all over the world, what is happening among Western countries today could happen for the entire world. People would be able to travel freely from one country to another without the need for a visa. People would then tend to think the same way all over the world, as there would be more and more contact between them. Since the standard of living would be the same and the political and economic systems would be very similar, the possibility of war between countries would be totally eliminated. The possibility of civil wars inside countries would be totally eliminated also, because civil wars are mostly caused by extreme poverty and misguided ideologies.

With global full harmony, we could achieve the condition of full material satisfaction and eternal peace all around the world, and the military budget could be totally eliminated. People living in full harmony would have nothing else to do but to love one another, and war would be no more.

Marshall Plan for Developing Countries

But how to quickly achieve full harmony all around the world? In previous chapters related to the elimination of poverty in developing countries, I discussed how rapid industrialization can be achieved in those countries with the help of the industrialization insurance provided by the Enermach Corporation. But with the great benefit that full harmony all over the world could bring to humanity, wouldn't it be interesting and exciting for the governments of developed countries to participate directly in the harmonization of the whole world?

To speed up the harmonization of the whole world, governments of developed countries could easily adopt an economic plan similar to the Marshall Plan adopted by the United States at the end of World War II to help rebuild devastated Europe.

For example, the government of the United States could adopt a plan of printing out of thin air $ 1 trillion each year and loaning that money to American companies with instructions to use it to create factories and services in developing counties. Although the money used in this program would be printed out of thin air, it would be quickly used to generate extra useful goods and services in developing countries. The US economy is highly efficient and complete, meaning that all sectors are highly developed. This means that the United States has the capability of quickly transforming that large amount of money into the machinery and equipment necessary to industrialize developing countries.

If enough money printed out thin air is loaned to a company that specializes in making cement, for example, this company could manufacture all the machinery and equipment needed to build a cement factory. The company could go ahead and build huge cement factories in developing countries of its choice. Since currency generated by the US government is accepted in all sectors of the US economy, this cement company would have no trouble paying its employees and suppliers for the work of building those factories.

The real question here would be whether the cement made in a given developing country would have buyers. This question is rather irrelevant, because money printed out of thin air would be loaned to thousands of US companies to help them create high-paying jobs in developing countries. Money would be loaned not only to cement companies but also to iron ore and steel companies, construction equipment companies, home appliances companies, home furnishing companies, farming companies, automobiles companies, textile companies, restaurants, hotels, banks, insurance companies, and retail sales companies. As all these companies would be coming to a given country at the same time, there would be millions of high-paying jobs created. In turn, all these companies would have customers for the products they manufacture or the services they provide.

This would be like building the economy of a country from scratch. The key strategy here is to start big from the very beginning. A very large amount of money would have to be printed out of thin air and loaned to companies with the instructions of starting new businesses at the same time in developing countries.

If a necessary raw material is abundant in any given country but is needed by other countries, a reasonable price for that commodity would be established so that other countries could easily have access to it. This wouldn't be a problem, because ultimately all countries of the world would achieve the same level of economic development. There would be no need for the price of that necessary commodity to skyrocket for the benefit of the producing country only.

Interestingly, this Marshall Plan for developing countries would never be a burden for the population of developed countries. It would rather create new opportunities, because millions of jobs would be created inside those countries, and salaries and wages would rise quickly as companies become bigger and make more profit from their operations overseas. I think this plan would even create a shortage of workers in developed countries, and it would be necessary to import unskilled workers from developing countries while exporting workers to developing countries to perform the high-skilled jobs being created there.

Another interesting fact about this plan is that companies that participate in this Marshall Plan for developing countries would not have to repay the loan given to them. All would have started with money printed out of thin air. Companies would be loaned money in order to build new capacity in developing countries, and once this new capacity was operational, there would be no need to repay the loan.

This is truly a new way of doing business, and it is possible because of all the industrial capabilities existing now on this planet and all the know-how that exists today in developed countries. The key here is to directly loan money printed out of thin air to companies that have the capability to transform it into useful goods and services. The population can then only have access to that money through working jobs. I believe that the old way of doing business—where a company starts small and spend years growing by means of the profit earned from its operations or by the appreciation of its share on the stock market—is long outdated.

This Marshall Plan for developing countries would have to be implemented wisely in order to ensure the expected results. For example, when dealing with a country under dictatorship or considered an enemy, it would be necessary not to ask for any concession or political change from the leadership of that country. The right strategy would be to engage the country purely on an economic level, and in a sincere and friendly way propose to the leaders of that country an industrialization package that will help end poverty. If the leadership realizes that you have no intention of destabilizing its regime and are only interested in helping to solve economic problems, I don't see how they could reject the help.

It would then be possible to start building factories and modern homes in that country. Millions of high-paying jobs would be created, and this would bring prosperity to the country and help the population escape the hardship caused by authoritarian rule. As economic conditions improved and the population became wealthier, it would be possible for more and more foreigners to visit the country. The people from that country would also have more and more opportunities to travel abroad. This would be possible because the leaders would no longer see any danger to letting people travel abroad, since the foreign countries visited would now be considered friends. In this way, material harmony and ideological harmony would be progressively achieved until the conditions for dictatorship are simply terminated.

For a country that is considered an enemy, the same strategy would be followed. The leaders of that country would be presented, in a friendly and sincere manner, with an industrialization package that would help end poverty. As the leaders of that country realize that you are promising economic prosperity and have no negative intentions, they would begin to change their opinion about you and, ultimately, consider you a friend. If they were developing sophisticated weaponry in order to defend themselves against you, certainly they would abandon those programs, because you would now be close friends. In this case, again, material harmony would lead to ideological harmony. The prospects of war would be completely eliminated.

Concerning conflicts based on faith or ideology, those tend to take place in countries characterized by widespread poverty. In the case of Islamic radicalism, for example, we can see that it has trouble taking root in prosperous Islamic countries like Qatar, UAE, Bahrain, and Kuwait. However, countries with fewer economic opportunities like Afghanistan, Pakistan, Iraq, Iran, Egypt, Lebanon, Syria, Libya, and Yemen tend to have socioeconomic conditions favoring extremist ideology.

Ask yourself where Islamic radicalism was during the Cold War. During that forty-five-year period, almost all conflicts around the world had roots in the conflict between the United States and the Soviet Union. Each country was trying to spread its ideology. Conflict between Capitalism and Communism was then the main cause of strife around the world, and Islamic fundamentalism was dormant.

Once the Cold War ended, Islamic fundamentalism found an opportunity to emerge, causing all kinds of problems, as we see today. If a new economic model could be implemented, there is no doubt that radical Islam would lose ground. People would rather be busy exploiting new opportunities to improve their lives.

In this way, the Marshall Plan for developing countries can easily lead to harmony all over the world. Once the living standards become almost the same and people are living under the same economic and political conditions, they will be able to travel freely and tend to think the same way. Since in the process of material harmonization countries would have helped each other through globalization, no country would consider another as an adversary or enemy. This would inevitably lead to peace all over the world.

A Money-less Society

I have mentioned that a perfect society on earth is a society where harmony, peace, and love reign. I have described harmony as having two aspects: material and ideological. Since harmony all over the world is what leads to peace and love among people, I will go into more detail about how to achieve full harmony.

Material harmony all over the world means that all the material needs of the people living in all countries of the world are fully met. The living standards in all countries of the world are the same. There is total prosperity everywhere.

Material harmony can, however, be difficult to achieve. The material needs of people and the wealth they dream of having before they will be satisfied is rather immense. For example, the salaries people are paid in their jobs are the highest in the United States, but still the American people are very unsatisfied. This is easily seen in the number of people who play the lottery, trying to become millionaires. As the jackpot grows bigger and begins to reach hundreds of millions of dollars, you see virtually everybody buying a lottery ticket, hoping to be the one to hit the jackpot, even if the chance of winning is extremely slim. Everyone would like to become a multimillionaire and even a billionaire, so that his material needs can be met.

Do we have to make every person on this planet a billionaire in order to achieve full material harmony? I think that the answer to this question is to instead create a society without money. You wouldn't have to buy or pay for anything you need. Whether you need a car or a house to live in, you would not have to pay anything to get it. You would just go to the location where new cars were stored for distribution, pick the one you like, and drive away with it. Should you need a new home to live in, you would look through catalogues, pick the home that you like, and move in without paying a dime.

When you wanted to get food or clothing, you would go to a grocery store or a department store and pick what you need, and walk away with it without paying anything. If you wanted to travel, you would just make a reservation and board an airplane to your destination. Once you got there, you wouldn't have to worry about anything, because everything would be free.

Eliminating money would allow everybody to have full access to any goods and services that exist on this planet. Every single person living on this planet would have the impression that he or she owns the whole planet, with full access to anything that exists on it. This would be much better than being a billionaire. I don't think there exist a billionaire who can pretend to own the whole planet.

Once a money-less society was achieved, crimes like robbery and corruption would simply be terminated. Services like banking and insurance would also cease to exist. They wouldn't be needed anymore.

But how to eliminate money and make a reality the dream of living in a money-less society? Obviously, the solution is not to simply eliminate money and hope that people will keep working their jobs. Many people would simply stop working, and those who kept working would find it unfair to be working while others have all that they needs while doing nothing. This solution would lead to a total collapse of the system and deep poverty.

The solution to this problem is technology. In previous chapters, I discussed how today's technology and know-how can lead to the development of an android with humanlike abilities. With the latest innovations in digital technology, I believe it is possible to develop an android that can perform almost any job that a human being can do.

There are really very few jobs that a highly developed android cannot do. For example, designing a brand new car model that would be aesthetically more beautiful than the previous model can never be achieved by an android or a supercomputer. I don't see how a computer can have a sense of beauty and style. This task is even difficult for humans. Engineers have been designing new cars for more than a century now, and there still are some cars that come out of production lines looking rather ugly and unappealing. Also, doing research to develop a brand-new drug or a new product line is not something that can be performed satisfactory by a computer alone.

Almost all other jobs performed by humans today can be done by a highly developed android. I think that if we began now to develop these kinds of androids for the purpose of taking over jobs done by humans today, we could have fully functioning humanoid androids within twelve years. These androids would work with little supervision in mining, farming, factories, construction, and services. If we could close the whole cycle of producing needed goods and services using androids, why would we then have to work at jobs? Why would we have to pay money for the goods and services we need? Simply put, everything would be free.

The key to substituting androids for humans would be to massively manufacture these smart androids and introduce them en masse and over a short period of time in the production of needed goods and services all over the world.

This way, we wouldn't have a situation where some people lose their jobs and unemployment becomes a problem. By introducing androids in the production of goods and services over a short period of time, we can quickly scale back the use of money, and the negative consequences of this process can be mitigated.

Smart androids would be programmed to build new houses and hotels, work in factories and in the farming sector, work in mining, and work in the service sector. Since androids can work twenty-four hours a day, seven days a week, productivity will be very high, and the amount of wealth generated will be immense. It will be possible to build millions of luxurious hotels all over the world and tens of thousands of luxurious cruise ships. People will spend their time travelling around the world, dining in fancy restaurants, and relaxing at the beach.

Once full material and ideological harmony is achieved, the poverty and isolationism that lead to wars and strife among countries and among people would be completely terminated. People could live peacefully and happily on this planet. The only thing they would have left to do is love one another.

By the year 2029—approximately when these smart androids will be ready—a high degree of harmony will have been achieved all over the world through the Marshall Plan for developing countries. There will have been a tremendous economic expansion all over the world. Companies will have generated huge profits, and the majority of people living on this planet will have made a large amount of money. The problem of money and wealth will have been substantially tackled.

Negative consequences of this money-less society

Since almost all jobs would be taken over by androids and a large percentage of the population would not have to work, there is still the question of who would do the necessary jobs androids cannot perform. I mentioned earlier the case of designing a brand new car model. Who would do the work of designing a brand new product while others relax on the beach?

It is clear that in this kind of economy, there would be no competition, and this would result in less research and development. There would be fewer and fewer new products coming to the market.

In order to stimulate people to still do some necessary work, a system of rewards can be established. For example, hotels could have a certain number of hotel suites especially refurbished to be much more luxurious than the rest of the hotel rooms. Everything in those special suites might be made of gold, for example, and you would have to have special permission to be able to use those highly luxurious suites. Someone who has agreed to do a job would have a special pass allowing access to these highly luxurious hotel rooms.

Similarly, some cars would be made different from the rest, with luxurious features ordinary cars do not have. Additional special products and rewards can be established, and only people who do some necessary work would have access to those products.

A large number of people could be trained to do the necessary jobs so that no one would need to work more than part-time—let's say a few weeks per year. The rest of the time, they would enjoy themselves like the rest of the population.

If we consider jobs like teaching students in classrooms or some health-care research jobs, we can see that by training a large number of people to do these jobs, almost everyone would only have to be available for a short period of time every year. Once someone finished performing his assigned job, he or she would be able to spend the rest of the year vacationing.

Given the pace of innovation and creativity observed today, I think that any product on the market will have reached a high degree of refinement and improvement fifteen years from now. Even if the product remained unchanged, it would continue to have acceptable qualities for a very long time. I do not believe that fifteen years from now, it will still be possible to substantially improve the iPhone, for example.

Given the huge benefits of a money-less society and the peace of mind that results from it, I think we can let go the benefit gained from constant competition and innovation, and choose rather to live in a peaceful word where we have total peace of mind, without worries about economic crises, poverty, wars, terrorism, corruption, stress, robberies, or material needs.

CONCLUSION

This new economic model based on introducing money printed out of thin air into the economy through modern home construction and furnishing creates millions of high-paying jobs and culminates in the eradication of poverty all over the world. No matter the size or population of any given country, no matter how severe the situation of poverty existing there, it would be possible to establish a home-building program that allows for ending poverty in just fifteen years.

If developed countries could adopt the Marshall Plan for developing countries, this would lead to rapid industrialization of developing countries, achieving material harmony all over the world.

Material harmony would lead to ideological harmony. Eternal peace all over the world would follow, and war would be no more. As smart androids began to take over jobs that were done by people, humans would have plenty of time to spend vacationing and enjoying themselves in an increasingly money-less society.

The only obstacle to this way of living would be energy. Current energy technologies have proven to be extremely expensive and also very hazardous to the environment and to the health of people. But with the invention of an energy machine, this problem will be resolved, and we will have the prospect of a future in a clean and safer world.

With this new economic model, it will be very easy to build thousands of highly luxurious hotels around the world and tens of thousands luxurious cruise ships, allowing people to live a truly luxurious and joyful life. Once smart androids become available, it would even be possible to build new cities that are very sophisticated and destroy old ones.

It would also be possible to put a halt to the destruction of important ecosystems like the tropical rain forests, as the people who were attacking them find a better way of living. Animal poaching can be stopped as well, and endangered species can recover and live in harmony with people.

Once full material harmony and full ideological harmony have been achieved all over the world and a money-less society has become a reality, every single person living on this planet will have the impression that he or she owns the whole planet. It will then seem like the whole world is made of a single country only. Conditions for wars, terrorism, dictatorships, economic crises, corruption, or any other kind of hardship will have been completely terminated. This does not mean that countries will lose their culture, however.

With this new economic model, it is clear that people will know now where humanity is headed, and the future wil look bright for the people living on the planet today and for future generations. If we start doing the right thing now, we can achieve a near perfect society on earth within fifteen years. By the year 2040, people on earth could be spending their time partying, traveling, dining at fancy restaurants, relaxing at the beach, going to sport events, jamming all the time, and simply living a life characterized mostly by joy and happiness.

Isn't this what the dream expressed by John Lennon through the song "Imagine" is all about?

HISTORY OF THE ENERGY MACHINE AND THE NEW ECONOMIC MODEL

I began doing research on the energy machine in 1984, when I was in the ninth grade in high school. I had just learned the principle of energy conservation, and I was surprised by the affirmation that energy cannot be created. I began doing research, and I remember trying a design that consisted of a wheel on which several falling masses were installed to transmit kinetic energy to the wheel by falling and spinning it. I quickly realized that this would not work.

In 1986, when I was in the eleventh grade, I was impressed by a phenomenon often called the hydrostatic paradox. As I analyzed it, I became convinced that I could use it to build a machine that would generate mechanical energy without consuming anything. Since then, I have tried numerous designs to try to exploit that phenomenon, but I could never escape the principle of energy conservation. Sometimes I would quit my research for months, feeling defeated, only to come back later and continue.

By 1993, I had come up with a design that would theoretically produce energy from gravity, but the machine had to be extremely big. I spent many more years trying to find a way to reduce the size of the machine, but without success.

In October 2003, I changed my approach to the problem, and things began to fall into place quickly. By December 2003, I had developed a design for an energy machine that I thought would successfully generate mechanical energy without consuming anything, and that could be of any size depending on the power output desired. I was able to build that machine, but there was an error in the concept, and the machine didn't work. From what I learned with the failed design, I came up with a new and successful design by December 2007. I am currently trying to find enough money to build a working model of the machine.

I knew that if I could successfully design a working machine, it could offer a great opportunity to tackle the problem of poverty around the world. I was born in Rwanda, one of the poorest countries in the world. As I grew up there, I kept asking myself whether it would ever be possible to solve the problem of extreme poverty existing there. Rwanda is a capitalist country with more than 12 million inhabitants today. Growing up there enabled me to analyze the vicious cycle of poverty and the difficulties that people face when trying to overcome it.

Later, I went to college in Cuba, a Communist country. While studying there, I could see firsthand the difficulties that Communist countries face when trying to solve the material needs of the population through planning, nationalization, and centralization.

After I arrived in the United States in 1995, I was able to analyze the economic model of that country. By comparing the three economic models (Rwandan, Cuban, and American), I was able to develop the economic model presented in this book. This new model mimics the economy of the United States, with the main difference being that, whereas in the United States people create new companies spontaneously and on their own, without the intervention of the federal government; in this new economic model the government is highly involved in the process of industrialization and does everything necessary to stimulate jobs creation.

ABOUT THE AUTHOR

Jean-Pierre Twagirayezu was born in Rwanda, Africa, in 1967. He attended a high school called College Saint-Andre located in Kigali, the capital of Rwanda, from 1981 to 1987. In high school, his majors were mathematics and physics. He followed an extensive course of mathematics and physics for six years, and many courses he took were college level.

After high school, he went to college in Cuba, where he majored in telecommunication engineering. In Cuba, he attended a university called ISAICC from September 1987 to July 1988 and learned Spanish there. From September 1988 to May 1990, he attended a university called ISPJAE. In college, he took extensive courses in mathematics and physics related to engineering.

He was unable to finish his degree because of an illness, and he returned to Rwanda in 1991. In 1994, he left Rwanda because of the civil war, and he was admitted as a permanent resident of the United States in 1995. Today he lives in the state of Virginia.

His main hobbies are music—mostly pop, rock, and reggae—but he also enjoys all kinds of music. He loves sports, especially ping-pong, soccer, tennis, volleyball, football and basketball. He also enjoys cartoon humor as well as movies in the genres of comedy, action, science fiction, and drama.